The Grateful Way

To Erin:

May you
live well
one T.H.X.
at a time!

The Grateful Way

FEEL FREE FROM REGRET IN THREE SMALL STEPS

IJ (IDA-JEAN) McINTYRE

Tellwell Talent
www.tellwell.ca

ISBN
978-0-2288-1143-5 (Hardcover)
978-0-2288-1142-8 (Paperback)
978-0-2288-1144-2 (eBook)

Table of Contents

In Memory

In loving memory of the most remarkable woman I have ever known,
my mom, Bernice Thomas Hanneson Neil
(1921 to 2011).

And in celebration of how she lived her life
as the epitome of the power of gratitude.

Many to Thank!

My book writing journey has been full of bonuses, for which I am exceptionally grateful.

I am indebted to a wise book coach, Les Kletke, who coaxed me to start even before I knew I had a whole book in me.

Thank you to my brother, Ken Hanneson and my sister, Karen (Hanneson) Saunderson for reading my first draft of the core stories, providing input and making this endeavour feel priceless.

During the writing of early versions of this book, the following people gave me positive encouragement and invaluable feedback for which I'm truly thankful:

- Cathie (Keiller) Godfrey and Debra Wallace in our post book writing boot camp *Best Seller Club*; plus:

- Anna Abra, Paul Abra, Lynda Clarke, Christine Dittaro, Rob Edwards, Laurie Flasko, Leslie Grant, Lynn Jeffery, Paul Krismer, Jeanne Martinson, Patricia Morgan, Jude Press, Nancy Prior, Graham Scholes, Marnie Scholes, Nell Smith, Deborah Turnbull and Susan Zerr.

Many thanks as well to my whole publishing team at Tellwell Talent; especially editor Helen Davies for understanding my intentions, sharing her impressions and providing constructive suggestions to make this book better.

And, lastly, a mountain of gratitude and an ocean of love to my husband for always being my biggest fan.

I could not have done this without all of you!

Thank you!

What's in this Book for You?

This book was inspired by the way my mom lived her life. So, yes, it's partly a tribute to her, but it is really about the power of gratitude.

Gratitude is not magic. It cannot, and does not, make miracles. Regret is inevitable in life. However, writing this book has taught me that living gratefully can soften regret.

Gratitude helps us focus on the positive, which can change the way we feel about what happens and encourage us to take simple, yet rewarding action.

When I look in my 'rear-view mirror', it's clear to me that only when I took individuals, opportunities and experiences in my life for granted have I felt regret. On the other hand, when I expressed my gratitude, I felt joy, love and relief—even in some of the most challenging moments of my life.

What's marvelous about gratitude is that everyone who expresses gratitude can experience its power. If you don't believe me, please check out the science. Starting on page 68 of this book are highlights from several studies that examine and confirm the benefits of actively practising gratitude.

This book shares the lessons I have learned about the nature of gratitude, illustrated by stories from the way Mom lived her life, together with my personal experiences.

After each chapter, you'll find an invitation for you to contemplate and commit to action entitled '*Your* **turn to take the wheel**'. These pages are designed to reinforce the steps you're already taking, add an idea or two to your repertoire and help you to enhance the benefits of living gratefully.

Writing this book, I realized there are times I have been a 'big talker' with good intentions, but good intentions are not enough; actions are what make a difference. It has become clear to me waiting for the perfect time doesn't work. What if there is no next time? So, I am committed to stop thinking without thanking.

Like everyone, I sometimes need nudges to get started. That's why I created a simple formula that helps me—three small steps:

1. *Take* **time to**
2. *H* **ighlight the positive, and,**
3. *X* **press gratitude.**

I invite you to take these three small steps—**T.H.X.**—to feel free from regret due to the power of living gratefully.

The Grateful Way to Live

Mom experienced many terrible times, including:

- Our house burning down when Dad was terminally ill;
- Without warning, her 37-year old son dying of a heart attack; and,
- Waking up in an Arizona hospital after suffering a stroke.

Did she give up? No! Even though she faced more than her fair share of tragedies, my mom was a 'glass half-full' optimist.

For most of my life I wondered: *How did she do it? How did she remain so positive? How did she manage to stay away from feeling regret?*

Finally, the answer came to me. She lived gratefully—no matter what. That's how she was able to stare adversity in the face, accept what she couldn't change, and find a way to move past the darkest moments of her life.

Gratitude also made the terrific times in Mom's life better. For example, she thoroughly appreciated:

- Being encouraged by her Arizona snowbird friends to take painting lessons when she was 61;
- Experiencing a fabulous European adventure with me when she was 64; and,
- Posing for three calendars when she was in her eighties (inspired by the movie, *Calendar Girls*). That's her at the wheel on the cover of this book!

Gratitude came naturally to Mom. Her simple and deliberate inclination to make the most of everything—terrible or terrific—served her well. She often said, "Where there's a will, there's a way." But not just *any* way. At each fork in the road my mom chose to take the *grateful* way. That's how she 'took the wheel' in her life's journey and made it such a remarkable trip.

Like most people, Mom had some regrets; but the key to her life was to take control of the things that could have dragged her down. That is the crux of this book. Understanding regret and rising above it is possible when we have a grateful attitude. Being thankful builds our confidence, optimism and courage.

May these true stories of addressing adversity and optimizing opportunities inspire you to live 'the grateful way'.

WHAT WOULD YOU SAVE?

When disaster strikes,
we discover what truly
matters.

Mom was born in 1921 on a farm near the town of Tisdale, Saskatchewan. My parents met when they were teenagers, while showing their prize-winning calves at the local fair, and it was love at first sight. In 1941 they married. Mom and Dad loved their life together, farming grain crops and tending livestock while raising four kids.

Our farmhouse did not have running water unless, as my mom joked, "We ran to the well to get it." No running water meant no indoor plumbing! The cook-stove in the kitchen was wood-burning and the furnace in the cellar was coal-fired. There was one large grate in the living room floor to heat the whole house.

Mom's days were spent cooking, baking, growing and canning vegetables, picking and selling berries, driving the tractor for the hay baler and driving the grain truck during harvest. She also worked in town, first as a hairdresser and then later as a dental assistant, and shared driving duties with my dad on a school bus route.

When not doing all those things, she sewed clothes for us kids as well as square dance outfits for her and my dad. Years later I learned I had completely embarrassed Mom one time, when, in an 'out of the mouths of babes' moment I proudly proclaimed to a group of our friends, "Mom sewed my new dress from an old pair of her pants!"

As a child, I had no idea how poor we were. It never even crossed my mind. We always had lots of delicious food to eat, nice clothes to wear and a home full of love—everything we needed and more.

My parents were active in the community. Mom and Dad curled in the winter, served the church and square danced whenever they could. In 1966, they were delighted when their friends in the Sasko Swinger Square Dance Club threw them a surprise party for their twenty-fifth wedding anniversary. Even though we didn't have much money, my parents felt like they had it all: a loving marriage, terrific kids and wonderful friends.

But 'having it all' didn't last. In 1968, less than two years after their special milestone anniversary celebration, Dad was diagnosed with stomach cancer. Surgery that fall to remove the tumour did not get all of it. By Christmas, he only had months to live.

That Christmas Eve, our family sang carols at the candlelight service at church. Then we spent the rest of the evening eating Mom's home-made peppermint patties and chocolate fudge while drinking eggnog by our beautifully decorated tree, with tinsel twinkling in the coloured lights. It was a peaceful, lovely time together as a family in our warm and cozy home.

When we woke up on Christmas morning, the house was frozen inside. Overnight, the coal fire had died. Normally, Dad would go to the cellar to get the fire going, but with him so ill it was Mom who did it this time. When she crawled back into bed beside my dad, she boasted, "I really got it going this time!"

My 18-year-old brother Oscar, who'd been sleeping on the living room sofa, was the first one up. At our house, presents delivered by Santa were never wrapped, so Oscar spotted his gift from Santa right away. Under the tree was the latest book about the Beatles! He immediately buried his nose in it.

As the youngest, at age eight, I bounded out of bed and saw a beautiful doll. I knew Santa had brought it just for me!

My 23-year-old sister Karen's two-year-old son, Kevin was thrilled to find a giant toy dump-truck with his name on it.

All three of us were delighted and preoccupied with our gifts—but when Mom came out to join us, all she could see were flames shooting out of the floor, higher than Oscar's head!

"FIRE!" she screamed.

Everyone sprang into action. Karen called the fire department while her husband Ken helped dress Dad and get him out of the house. Oscar ran to the well and back, and started dousing the flames with buckets of water. Mom rolled the flour bin from the kitchen into the living room and dumped close to one hundred pounds of flour on the flames. Everything happened so fast—but thankfully, all of us got out safely. Mom's quick action of throwing flour on the fire slowed it down so none of us were harmed.

Our house, unfortunately, was destroyed. The farm was two miles from town, so even though the volunteer firefighters contained the blaze, the water in the fire trucks' tanks wasn't enough to save it. Neighbours did their best to help retrieve our furnishings and belongings, but we lost practically everything. Anything that wasn't burned was badly damaged by smoke and water.

When this disaster struck, Mom couldn't believe it. She felt crushed and wanted to know … *Why is this happening to us? Clifford is dying of cancer. Isn't that enough? We're good people. Why are we being punished?*

But perhaps there was a reason. As it turned out, because of the fire, my family was forced to move off the farm before my dad passed away. It gave Dad tremendous comfort to know that Mom, Oscar and I were settled and secure in a house in town. Even though the fire destroyed our house and almost all that was inside it, we did not lose our 'home'—because our 'home' was wherever we were together as a family.

Fire Damages Hanneson Home Christmas Day

Fire extensively damaged the interior of the farm home of Mr. and Mrs. Cliff Hanneson near Tisdale Christmas morning. The blaze was brought under control by members of Tisdale Fire Department.

It might seem somewhat odd, but after the crisis passed, Mom was almost grateful we had that fire. She trusted that a higher power had been looking after us. In an unusual way, it was an exceptional Christmas gift.

Ultimately, Mom was just thankful we were safe, and she counted her blessings. She was grateful for the friends, neighbours and family who did all they could to help; she appreciated that we had insurance; and, she came to realize that losing the house was nothing compared to losing Dad. His cancer was what truly mattered, and it put the fire into perspective. Her gratitude for what we *did* have helped her get through the event and be there for Dad in his final days—which came far too soon.

For me: As a child, I didn't really understand the full power of counting blessings. I had no personal experience comparable to what Mom went through until my husband and I were evacuated in June 2013 as Calgary's raging, rising Bow River threatened to flood our house. Upon being alerted to the danger, we only had a couple of hours to pack our bags and run from room to room doing what we could to protect our belongings. It seemed we made hundreds of frantic trips from our basement to the second floor, all the time wondering, *why are our computers, important documents and priceless photographs all downstairs?*

When we loaded our car, locked the door and left behind our life, it was deeply distressing. For two long days and nights, we anxiously waited for word that we could return to our house. I was so afraid—even thinking about it now brings tightness to my chest. However, we ended up being extremely lucky; the path of the flood waters subsided half a block away from where we lived, so our house and possessions were spared.

At first, I was relieved and then I was thoroughly grateful. I also came to realize that even if our house *had* been flooded, our home—the love and life I share with my husband—would not have been destroyed. All our possessions could have been replaced. Losing our photographs would not have erased our memories.

Further, just as my parents had marveled at the community support after the fire, I marveled at how Calgarians rallied to help one another recover from the devastation. The selfless concern and support shown by complete strangers was unbelievably heartwarming. The worst disasters sometimes bring out the best in people—another blessing to count.

When disaster strikes, we discover what truly matters. Dealing with disaster is never easy. However, it makes us consider what we treasure the most. And, if we 'count our blessings', it's a gift that keeps on giving.

Your turn to 'take the wheel'

One way to deal with adversity is to **COUNT** your blessings. Focus on what you have, what makes you feel fortunate, and what you cherish—even the tiniest things.

List them one by one below, or create a mental list. You can do this anytime, such as when you're sitting in traffic, waiting in line at the grocery store, before you fall asleep or first thing in the morning when you wake up.

When you **COUNT** your blessings, you will discover that gratitude is a gift that keeps on giving.

Three small steps (T.H.X.)
to feel free from regret:

1. Take time to
2. Highlight the positive, and.
3. Xpress gratitude.

WHO WOULD YOU CALL?

When a friend is on our mind, the perfect time to call is now.

Mom and Dad were active square dancers. Whenever they could, as soon as the farm chores were done, they'd jump in the car and drive—often many miles and sometimes overnight—to have a fantastic time square dancing with fabulous friends.

Mom made their matching outfits, often hemming her skirt or sewing buttons on Dad's shirt at the last minute in the car on their way to a dance. By dancing to 100 different square dance callers in both Canada and the United States, they became members of the prestigious Century Club, an honour that they treasured.

Mom loved dancing with her tall man and Dad loved his beautiful partner just as much. When another dancer told Dad, "Bernice has great legs," Dad's reply was, "I know!"

When my parents' square dance friends heard about the fire on the farm, they wanted to help. Money was tight and the insurance coverage didn't go very far, so one frozen January night the Sasko Swingers (Mom and Dad's home club) held a benefit dance to raise funds for our family. Dancers from far and wide packed the Tisdale Civic Centre. Crinoline skirts rustled to the rhythm of the music and the men stepped lively in their crisp, western-style shirts and bolo ties.

> Allemande left with your left hand,
> Back to your partner for a right and left grand,
> Ace of Diamonds, Jack of Spades,
> Meet your partner and all promenade!

One of the best square dance callers in Western Canada, Earl Park—who was known for his elegant style and his velvet voice—came to call a few sets that night. As a special treat, he had a new dance to teach the crowd. Somewhat ironically, the new dance was called 'Red Hot', which wasn't lost on those who had gathered to help my family recover from our housefire.

> Promenade with the girl you've got,
> Shoot the star and go red hot,
> Men star left, whirl 'em away,
> Pass your girl and go red hot.

Off to the side of the stage, my parents watched with gratitude. I'll never forget the look on Dad's face. He was too ill to dance but, as his spirits were lifted by the outpouring of friendship, his eyes shone brightly.

Four months later the same friends who signed the guest book at that benefit dance returned for Dad's funeral. If not for the fire and the subsequent dance, my dad would never have had the opportunity to say goodbye to his many friends. It was a silver lining for Mom and Dad.

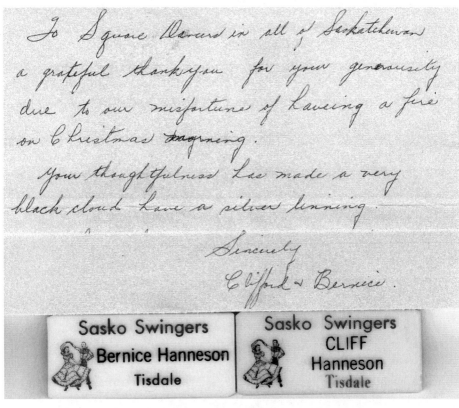

To Square Dancers in all of Saskatchewan a grateful thankyou for your generousity due to our misfortune of haveing a fire on Christmas morning.

Your thoughtfulness has made a very black cloud have a silver linning.

Sincerely
Clifford & Bernice.

Sasko Swingers
Bernice Hanneson
Tisdale

Sasko Swingers
CLIFF
Hanneson
Tisdale

Note of thanks Mom published in Saskatchewan newspapers.

For me: At eight years old, I was too young to appreciate the importance of taking time to connect with friends. I did not understand how powerful it must have been for Dad to see all those people and touch base with them before he died.

Years later, I understood.

There she was, my childhood friend, in a magazine! She was in an advertisement for a local television station and she looked amazing. I smiled as I ripped the page out and thought, *I'm so thrilled for her—I'll call.* But I didn't.

Sometime later, in one of those 'isn't it a small world?' conversations, my friend's name came up and once again I thought, *oh, yes, I must get in touch.* I made a note to phone her. But I didn't.

The next time I saw her name, it was in her obituary. I was thunderstruck. It was too late to call and all I could think was, *I can't believe she's gone! Why didn't I call?*

I attended her memorial service and paid my respects, but it was too late. Had I called, I would have known she was married, that she had twins, that she was ill. It still makes my heart hurt whenever I think about not picking up the phone. I deeply regret that I fell into the trap of waiting for a perfect time to get in touch. We were only in our forties. I had no idea time was running out while I was caught up in my own life.

Now, whenever something reminds me of a friend (be it a song or something else that jogs my memory), I take time to make a call and say, "I'm thinking of you. I'm glad we're friends."

I never regret calling. I only regret *not* calling.

When a friend is on our mind, the perfect time to call is now. Reaching out to say 'We care' warms hearts, lifts us up and prevents potential regret.

Your turn to 'take the wheel'

Take a moment to write down the name of one or more close friends who you haven't talked to for a while. Better yet, pick up the phone and **CALL right now** to let them know you're thinking of them. Tell them what they mean to you and how grateful you are to have them in your life.

CALL when you're thinking of someone! Start with one call—today.

You won't be sorry you did, and the friend you call will be grateful.

. . . .

Three small steps (T.H.X.)
to feel free from regret:

1. **T**ake time to
2. **H**ighlight the positive, and,
3. **X**press gratitude.

WHAT WOULD YOU ACCEPT?

When we can't control what's happening, knowing that love is eternal helps us find peace.

*T*hree small, new potatoes—*fresh from the garden* ... it was August 1968 when Dad left them on his plate and Mom knew immediately that something must be wrong. Only a few weeks before, he'd had a full physical exam as a requirement for his school bus driver's license, and everything had checked out ... but Dad not having an appetite was alarming.

What could it be?

Back to the doctor they went. This time, the doctor ordered several tests. When the results were in, he wanted to see both my parents. *This can't be good,* thought Mom. And it wasn't. Dad had stomach cancer. He needed surgery right away. He was only 54 years old.

Dad was the oldest of six children of Edgar and Ida Hanneson, who lived and farmed just outside of Tisdale. As a child, Dad attended a one-room school, and though he was incredibly smart and would have excelled at college, there was no money for him to go. As was customary those days, with only a grade eight education, he left school to work on the family farm.

His lack of formal education never hindered him. Everyone thought highly of Dad, whether he was skipping a winning curling team, contributing to the church board of directors or selling livestock at the auction market.

Dad had an attitude of 'que sera, sera' (what will be, will be), which he learned from being a farmer all his life. On the farm, you could never count on the weather, so you had to 'go with the flow'. Dad carried this sentiment over to how he dealt with his cancer.

It was not that way for Mom, though. When she heard the doctor say 'cancer', she was in shock. *No, it can't be! Yes, he smokes, but he has stomach cancer, not lung cancer!*

"Why you?" Mom cried out! "You're a family man, a community leader and a good guy! You don't even drink!"

Dad quietly answered, "Why not me?"

What could Mom say to that? What could anyone say to an attitude like that?

That was Dad's way, the way he approached what he couldn't control and the way he accepted the news his life would soon end. Thankfully, his acceptance gave both him and Mom some peace and helped them get through this difficult time.

My parents both felt Dad had lived his life well. More importantly, he had no regrets. It gave profound solace to both of them to know they had loved each other so deeply. They were grateful for the years they had enjoyed together and so, rather than allowing denial or anger to take hold, they accepted what was happening with serenity, which gave dignity to Dad in his dying days.

Twenty-fifth wedding anniversary.

For me: As a child, watching how my parents handled my dad's cancer diagnosis and death was a particularly good lesson in acceptance. After Dad was gone, there were many times when an adult, upon meeting me, asked the standard question, "What does your dad do?"

I would answer, "My dad died when I was nine," quite matter-of-factly.

I vividly recall the awkward silences that followed. I learned that many people are uncomfortable and at a loss for words when they find out you have lost someone dear, especially if they have not yet experienced the death of someone close. But, thanks to the grace with which my parents handled this situation, I came to see my dad's death as a fact of life, something that I could not change. This allowed me to accept it and to move on.

Perhaps even before I was conscious of it, I realized that my dad's cancer was beyond my control. I also realized that his death could not take away the love he felt for Mom, my brothers, my sister and me. I knew he wasn't leaving us willingly. Even at the very end, the touch of his hand, his weak smile, the loving look in his eyes showed us how much he cared, and that his affection for all of us would last forever.

*When we can't control what's happening,
knowing that love is eternal helps us find peace.
Losing a loved one is extremely difficult. Learning
to accept what we cannot change and showing
gratitude for the love we will always have in our
heart, grants us serenity.*

Your turn to 'take the wheel'

A wonderful way to express gratitude is to **SHOW** you're grateful with gestures, like a smile, a wave, a hug or a squeeze of a hand. Sometimes gestures are even better than words. Small gestures can make a big difference.

Jot down a few ideas below about times when, places where and people who you will express your thanks to, or **SHOW** your love for, with simple gestures like these. Saying 'thanks' the next time you're on the *receiving* end of such a gesture will also fill your heart.

. . . .

Three small steps (T.H.X.)
to feel free from regret:

1. Take time to
2. Highlight the positive, and,
3. Xpress gratitude.

HOW WOULD
YOU GO ON?

*When faced with an unexpected
challenge, believing in a positive
purpose helps us handle it.*

Dad was the love of Mom's life. They had just celebrated their twenty-seventh wedding anniversary and were looking ahead to many more years together when in nine short months, it all ended.

Even though on one level, Mom had come to accept Dad's death from cancer, when reality hit, she was devastated. She felt like collapsing with grief; drowning her sorrows in a bottle; succumbing. But she couldn't give up. She had to pull through. She had to go on—for me. I was only nine years old and she knew I needed her.

When my parents first married, my mom wanted four kids. She dreamed of having, in this order, 'boy, girl, boy, girl'. In the 1940s and 1950s first she gave birth to Ken, then Karen, then Oscar, and she thought that was it. But nine years later Mom found out she was pregnant with me. In that sense, I was an 'afterthought'. Although a fourth child had been in Mom's initial plans, she'd long given up on giving birth to another baby!

As ultrasound was not yet available, there was no way to know whether she was pregnant with a boy or a girl—so Mom had no idea what to expect.

When Dr. Wright delivered me, he exclaimed, "It's a girl!" Mom could not believe it. She was so sure her wish of 'boy, girl, boy, girl' would not come true.

Finally, the nurse said to Dr. Wright, "Well, show her!" And indeed I was a baby girl!

Years later, Mom shared with me her belief that I was put on this earth to make sure she didn't fall apart after Dad died. She told me she didn't know what she would have done if it hadn't been for me; she might have just given up.

When Dad passed away, the two oldest kids, Ken and Karen had already left home, while the youngest boy in the family, my brother Oscar, was in grade 11 and getting ready to make his way in the world. A year later, after graduating, he went off to university in Regina leaving Mom and me alone.

After my dad died, Mom felt like she had no reason to get out of bed—except for me; for that reason, she was thankful that she had to look after someone. Instead of dwelling on being unexpectedly widowed, she found purpose in being a mom. Positive purpose stopped her from wallowing in the depths of her sorrow.

My first making-ends-meet lessons were at our kitchen table. With no one else around, I was the one Mom talked to about running the farm, paying the bills and making the mortgage payments on our house in town. She asked questions like, "Should I take an offer for cash rental or a crop-share arrangement for the farm?" "Which local retail store should I work at: Robinson's or Pearson's?" "Should I finish the basement and rent out a suite?"

I didn't have any answers, and she didn't expect them. She just wanted a sounding board so she could sort out what she would do.

While I was growing up, my mom and I mostly got along extremely well—though there were certainly moments when I'm sure my being a typical, independent, impulsive teenage girl made her question whether my birth was such a good thing after all! But, because those rough patches couldn't begin to compare with losing Dad, it was fairly easy for her to keep them in perspective, and so we were always able to put them behind us pretty quickly.

Whether or not I was 'sent for a reason' as my mom believed, faith in this got her through countless dark, difficult days and long, lonely nights. She had to keep it together for her youngest child. She was truly grateful for having a positive purpose; it gave her a reason and the strength to go on.

A
Daughter
is a
Special Gift

I thought the valentine rather
special as you were the gift
we hadn't looked for!!!

Don't know what I would have
done without ~~you~~ — even this
Christmas time.

Love
Mum,

For me: At first, catching sight of anything good coming from my dad's death was practically impossible. To this day, I wish I could have had him in my life longer—but I do love that the situation resulted in an especially strong bond with my mom.

Living together, just the two of us, for eight years (before I headed off to university) created a unique, beautiful mother-daughter relationship. We remained close for the rest of her life, sharing much love, joy and gratitude. Celebrating special occasions together whenever possible, we often presented carefully chosen cards with added personal notes—reinforcing our mutual appreciation.

When faced with an unexpected challenge, believing in a positive purpose helps us handle it. Communicating appreciation—in person—to those who have helped us 'go on' is especially meaningful.

Your turn to 'take the wheel'

A powerful way of expressing gratitude is to write a message of appreciation and then share your thanks in a face-to-face **VISIT**. Get together over a cup of coffee or a glass of wine. If it's impractical to meet in person, schedule a video call.

Start with one special person. Write a 'thank you' letter or note, set up a time and place for your **VISIT**, read your message out loud and then present your letter or note. This will have a lasting, uplifting impact on both you and the person you are thanking. It may inspire you and/or the recipient to write and present messages of appreciation to others as well.

Three small steps (T.H.X.)
to feel free from regret:

1. **T**ake time to
2. **H**ighlight the positive, and,
3. **X**press gratitude.

WHAT WOULD YOU DECIDE?

When change is imposed on us,
being thankful for possibilities
helps us decide what's best.

O n especially cold, snowy, winter evenings Mom and Dad would head down the hill from the farm to have the neighbour read their tea leaves. One night, Mrs. Pearce gazed at the pattern inside Mom's teacup and unexpectedly said, "You will have a second husband."

Mom emphatically replied, "There's no way!"

It was impossible for Mom to imagine she would ever be anything other than 'Mrs. C.A. Hanneson'. That's who she was, who she was happy to be and who she wanted to be forever. But years later, the message in the tea leaves came true.

A widow at only 47, Mom was still young when dad died. Dad's life had ended, but hers had not. My mom worked at a shop in town. A man named Bordie Neil owned a clothing store down the street from where she was working. When they ended up at the National Café at the same time on coffee breaks, they started to share their experiences. Cancer had also taken Bordie's spouse, so they had something life-changing in common.

For Mom and Bordie, being able to open up about what each of them had gone through was healing. They had experienced the same pain, each in their own way. It helped each of them to be able to talk with someone who understood what it was like to watch a beloved spouse die. This 'coming together' paved the way to a new relationship, though they both faced fears about starting over.

Bordie was out-going, good-natured and loved to laugh—just like my dad. However, though everyone knew Mom and Bordie were dating, because they each came from different social circles in Tisdale, the two of them weren't automatically seen as a couple by either of their previous groups of friends.

Mom didn't play bridge. Bordie didn't square dance. And so 'Bernice and Bordie' as a unit didn't quite fit.

It was awkward for them and difficult—or so it seemed—for their friends to accept them as a 'pair'. Some friends even seemed to disapprove, and Mom wondered if those friends thought it was too soon for her to find another partner. Other friends were simply still in the habit of expecting 'Bernice and Clifford' or 'Bordie and Eleanor'. For people in Tisdale to accept 'Bernice and Bordie' would take time.

By 1977, when I left to study sociology and law in Saskatoon, Mom was 55 and Bordie was 66. They were ready to enjoy life together in retirement—and so they got married. After a lovely family wedding, they honeymooned in Mesa, Arizona. There, they liked the Holiday Village Mobile Home Park so much that they bought their own place before returning to Saskatchewan the following spring.

At the Holiday Village Mobile Home Park, not only was the warm winter weather delightful, they made new friends as a couple. No one in Holiday Village knew them as anything other than 'Bordie and Bernice'. Here, they belonged. Here, they fit in. Second marriages because of death or divorce were common among their new snowbird friends and so they were completely accepted. It was magic.

Becoming part of this new community was wonderful for Mom and Bordie—Holiday Village gave them a fresh start. They were not identified by their past or defined as 'coming from the farm' or 'living in town'. They had no 'past lives' to get in the way. They could, and did, create a whole new life together.

At Holiday Village, both Mom and Bordie swam every day—Mom without ever getting her hair wet! Mom also learned how to play bridge with her new friends, something Bordie used to enjoy with his first wife. He never took up square dancing, but 'Bordie and Bernice' never missed an old-time dance, and that was just as much fun for my mom.

Both Mom and Bordie were grateful for their first spouses, marriages and families; however, neither of them dwelt in the past. Neither Mom nor Bordie expected to lose their spouse, or to have a second marriage—yet they felt fortunate to have found each other, as well as a new set of friends and a place where they belonged. They believed it was up to them to choose how to live after the loss of their spouses, and they were thankful they did.

For me: While Mom and Bordie were creating their new life together, I convocated, articled and became a lawyer. Five years later, my position as a Crown prosecutor was unexpectedly downsized as part of 2,000 budget cuts one 'black Tuesday' in May, 1987. Initially, I was completely shocked, but very quickly I felt I would be just fine, and I was right. It helped me to know my job was eliminated because my boss was confident I'd have other opportunities. He was right. I received an offer from a law firm specializing in criminal litigation the very same day and even though it happened 'out of the blue', it gave me the chance to consider new possibilities.

When I chose to give up the practice of law, several friends and relations did not understand. In their eyes, being a lawyer was my identity. But today, as a workshop facilitator, conference speaker, and author, all the reasons I pursued a law degree in the first place have come together. Helping people and making a difference has been a more rewarding career for me than law.

At my core, I'm an advocate rather than an adversary, and so encouraging others to see positive potential fits me well.

When change is imposed on us, being thankful for possibilities helps us decide what's best. No one can define us unless we let them. Too often we are defined by the past, but we are more than where we come from, what we do, or who we married. Thankfully, we get to choose.

Your turn to 'take the wheel'

Is there someone in your life who has been there for you, encouraging you when you were going through a time of change? Is there someone who pointed you toward possibilities when you could not see them yourself?

Below, list those you will **SEND** a note of thanks (handwritten or via email). A thank you card is a great way to acknowledge kindness shown, or support given, as you make decisions that are right for you.

. . . .

Three small steps (T.H.X.)
to feel free from regret:

1. Take time to
2. Highlight the positive, and.
3. Xpress gratitude.

WHAT WOULD
YOU TRY?

*When self-doubt gets in our
way, supportive friends will
encourage us.*

The autumn she was 61, Mom began to paint in oils with palette-knives. Almost overnight, in Art Kerner's classes, her talent came to life, and she captured on canvas landscapes ranging from the red rock and cacti of Arizona to the parkland lakes, trees and snowdrifts of northern Saskatchewan. Later, after studying with two more Arizona artists, she added delicate floral paintings, including sheer roses, to her repertoire. She was an artist—and a good one.

The hours she spent painting beautiful images on canvas were extremely satisfying to her. She even made a little money from selling her paintings, but the true bonuses were the pleasure and accolades she received from gifting paintings to friends, family, fans and good causes across Canada and the United States, plus the honour she felt when her granddaughter, Kara-Lyn, presented seven paintings to her host families in Japan on a Rotary Student Exchange.

Mom was further pleased to display her pieces in several galleries and art exhibitions, of which the annual Tisdale Arts Group Show and Sale was a favourite. By tradition it was held on the Mother's Day weekend and I loved making the trip home to be there as a tremendously proud daughter: *That's my mom!*

Many people expressed amazement at how she had discovered her talent so late in life. I was delighted to hear people ask her, "Wow, how do you do it?"

It was uplifting and inspiring to see her encourage others to take painting lessons and try it themselves. Mom was especially thrilled to receive 'The People's Choice Award' on several occasions, signifying how much her art resonated with those who attended the show. It meant even more to her when someone bought a painting; that was the sincerest compliment.

Like most overnight success stories, looking back, it's not surprising Mom was a gifted painter. Mom always expressed herself creatively in one way or another. She stitched many petit point and needle point treasures; she made copper-tooled lamps and leather-tooled wallets; she arranged flowers beautifully ... and then there was all the knitting she did, often without a pattern!

Even though she was introduced to painting in water colours by three local Tisdale artists in the months after Dad's death, the timing for her was not yet right. It was years later, when her snowbird friends encouraged her, that she was able to give it a try. All it took was to get started, and then she was hooked.

Thanks to her Arizona friends coaxing her to go with them to take some lessons, Mom enjoyed much success as an artist—all because she decided to go ahead and try. She was so thankful to them for helping her see how to experiment!

In the 1980s, when Mom started painting, she was already in her 60s. People her age were considered to be 'senior citizens' and definitely that title was official at 65. But instead of thinking, 'I'm too old to learn how to paint,' Mom, with the help of her persuasive friends, decided to be open to doing something new and was willing to give it a chance. If she didn't at least try, how would she ever know if painting was something she might truly love?

Though she was a confident, creative woman she initially hesitated to take that first step as she, like so many of us, no doubt had fears of failure. *I've never done anything quite like this. I don't know if I can paint as well as my friends. What if I'm not good at it?*

Thankfully, she put aside her fears and signed up for one lesson. If painting wasn't for her, she reasoned, it would be just fine to quit. And even though her very first oil painting, a landscape scene of a lake painted in three lessons, wasn't perfect (she always thought it looked like the water was going to fall out of the lake and off the wall!) she was still extremely happy with her initial effort.

That first painting was one of her personal treasures; it was a symbol of what can happen if you take a chance and just begin. Her talent and passion were revealed, and she came to life in a brand new way.

If Mom had not explored painting, her potential would have been left undiscovered and she would never have experienced being an artist. She would never have proudly handed out her first-ever business cards for 'Snowbird Studios' (designed by my sister for Mom's sixty-fourth birthday).

SNOWBIRD STUDIOS

Bernice Neil
Artist

1311 - 96th St.   425 - 701S. Dobson Road
P.O. Box 1803
Tisdale, Saskatchewan   Mesa, Arizona
S0E 1T0   85202
306-873-2336   602-834-6167

And, her family would not have her paintings as extraordinary reminders of how it's never too late to try something new.

Mom was so thankful for the support of good friends. With their encouragement, she found the confidence to try something new, and experience abundant joy with her painting.

The artist in her Arizona studio.

For me: In a similar way, my husband—who is my closest friend—encouraged me to resign from a well-paid, corporate human resources management position to start my own workshop facilitation business when I was 43 years old. I admit, I wasn't sure I had what it takes to be a successful entrepreneur.

Thankfully, with the help of friends who have their own businesses, and support from my colleagues at the Canadian Association of Professional Speakers, I flourished when I began designing and delivering life planning workshops and conference sessions.

In addition, being my own boss gave me the flexibility to make spending time with Mom my top priority during the last eight years of her life—a precious benefit.

It's almost impossible to describe the depth of my gratitude to my husband for his wholehearted support.

When self-doubt gets in our way, supportive friends will encourage us. It's okay to be scared. Just remember—it's never too late to try something new. We might succeed, or even excel! If we don't try, we may be left wondering, 'what if?'

Your turn to 'take the wheel'

Has anyone helped you overcome a fear you have had, or gain the courage to try something new? Is there something you would not have tried, or couldn't have done, if it weren't for one or more supportive people?

One way to show your appreciation is to **GIVE** support and encouragement to them in return. There may be something that they have not tried or been able to do without you! Make a note and reach out soon.

Three small steps (T.H.X.)
to feel free from regret:

1. Take time to
2. Highlight the positive. and.
3. Xpress gratitude.

WHAT WOULD YOU DO?

When opportunity comes along,
'going for it' prevents looking
back and wishing we had.

I can't recall when we first talked about it. I don't even remember if it was Mom or me who came up with the idea ... but we decided to take a trip to Europe. It was before the Internet and do-it-yourself holiday planning, so we went to see a travel agent. Then we researched every brochure looking for the best itinerary. *How could we go everywhere, see all the sights and do everything?*

I was single and had been working for the Saskatchewan Department of Justice for a few years. I had saved as many days as possible in my time-off bank and when I shared with my boss that I was booking a trip with my mom, he approved my vacation carry-over application. I had enough time off to travel overseas for six weeks!

After months of planning, on May 21, 1986 Mom and I flew from Saskatoon, Saskatchewan to London, England on a Wardair charter flight. Even though we weren't in first class, we felt like it! Wardair pampered us as if we were queens. Our tray-tables were covered with crisp, white tablecloths and our delicious dinners were presented on Royal Doulton china and served with chilled champagne.

"Bon voyage!" we toasted as we clinked our glasses.

Neither of us slept a wink during our flight; we were too excited! When we landed at London's Gatwick airport, even though it was three-thirty in the morning Saskatchewan time, Mom had fun flirting with two London bobbies. I snapped her photo with them.

The same bobbies showed us where to catch the train into the city and, when we arrived at London's Victoria Station, I suggested we hail a cab to our hotel, but my 64-year-old mom insisted, "We should take the tube!"

We figured out where to buy tickets, how to find the platform and caught the tube to High Street Kensington Station. There, we asked a Londoner for directions and were told we could walk to our hotel from there. He was kind enough to tell us about a shortcut through the Boots Drug Store, which we were grateful for. Our huge suitcases didn't have roller wheels (as they were not yet common) and we had both packed the largest bags allowed on our tour. After all, it was a six-week-long trip!

We checked in at the London Tara Hotel, went for a stroll and grabbed a bite to eat; then we were back on the tube, off to the New London Theatre. When making our travel arrangements, one of the first things we'd booked was a pair of tickets to the musical *CATS*.

On our way to the theatre, we briefly wondered if jet lag might catch up to us, worrying, *what if we fall asleep during the show?* Delightfully, the performance was exhilarating! Our front row seats put us right in the middle of the action, so there was no risk of nodding off! Rum Tum Tugger was Mom's favourite character, but all the actors, music, costumes and choreography were unforgettable.

At five o'clock the next morning our alarm went off, and by six we were showered, dressed and packed. We put our suitcases outside our hotel room door and headed downstairs to have breakfast with our travel companions. Immediately, we made friends with Mary, Wilma and Josie, three sisters from Melbourne, Australia.

We would spend the next 23 days on Trafalgar's Grand European tour, followed by six days exploring London on our own, and capped off with a 12-day Britain and Ireland tour. Yes, they were the kind of bus tours everyone jokes about; 'if it's Tuesday, it must be Belgium' ... though we were actually in Belgium on Saturday and Sunday. But you get the picture!

With everything all taken care of, we sat back, relaxed and enjoyed every minute of sightseeing. As the tour brochure advertised, 'Once upon a time, the *Grand Tour of Europe* was a must for fashionable society. See why, as you travel in Trafalgar luxury.' Yes, we visited all the typical, touristy sights and it was sublime!

In St. Moritz, Switzerland we stayed in the charming Hotel Neus. During our delicious dinner, it started to snow! The Australians loved it. They had never seen snow before. The next thing I knew we were all outside, and Mom was in the middle of the action throwing snowballs!

We saw spectacular sights, such as the Sistine Chapel, the Eiffel Tower and Edinburgh Castle. Everywhere we went, we loved the breathtaking scenery, the amazing history and the friendly people. We never forgot getting into the Van Gogh Gallery in Amsterdam for free because we were Canadian, laughing until we cried at Irish comic Hal Roach's jokes in Dublin and savouring the elegance of high tea at the Savoy Hotel in London on the last day of our trip.

Mom felt so fortunate to have these opportunities. There was never a time when she hesitated to take part, not even for a second. She tasted everything, from frog's legs in France, to Guinness in Ireland, to haggis in Scotland. She twisted backwards into a pretzel to kiss the Blarney Stone, climbed the 294 steps to the top of the Leaning Tower of Pisa and flattened herself on the bottom of the row boat in the Blue Grotto on the Isle of Capri.

Because Mom was always willing to 'go for it', she was never left wondering what she might have missed.

Throwing coins into Rome's Trevi Fountain.

For me: That whole trip, I was in awe of Mom. Travelling together brought the two of us even closer and I ended up with a whole new appreciation of Mom as a woman. She was so energetic and adventurous, and she never wanted to miss anything. She wasn't a classic 'senior citizen' in any way, shape or form! I realized I truly admired her. She lived and loved life to the fullest, an example I committed to follow.

When Mom and I were in Rome, we threw our coins into Trevi Fountain and we both made a wish. Mine was to be just like her. It was a moment I will never forget.

When opportunity comes along, 'going for it' prevents looking back and wishing we had. Sometimes we shy away from unfamiliar places or unfamiliar people. Being grateful helps us push past our comfort zones, making our travels richer and more memorable.

Your turn to 'take the wheel'

In your travels, be they near or far, take the time to focus on what you're noticing. Then, jot down even just one thing you're thankful you experienced. **WRITE** your thoughts on this page, in a journal, in a travel album, using an app on your personal device … or simply make notes and pop them into a 'gratitude jar' to preserve your memories.

Later, re-reading your notes will take you back, reviving your best souvenirs—unforgettable moments.

Three small steps (T.H.X.)
to feel free from regret:

1. Take time to
2. Highlight the positive, and,
3. Xpress gratitude.

WHAT WOULD YOU SHARE?

When we share our wishes,
we make it easier for loved ones
should something happen to us.

As a youngster, my brother Oscar was accident-prone. One time when he was riding on the tractor with our dad, he fell off the back and was run over by one of the huge rear tires. Dad, extremely distraught, scooped him up and ran to the house. Both my parents jumped in the car and drove the two miles to the hospital.

After 17 days in hospital, the doctor confirmed Oscar didn't have any serious internal injuries. Thankfully, the deep snow in the field, and Oscar's thick snowsuit, protected him.

Another time, Oscar put his hand through the glass door of Mom's china cabinet. Blood was flying everywhere. Our sister Karen grabbed a towel and wrapped it tightly around the jagged cut on his arm. Again, Dad drove the two miles to the hospital. Several stitches and a few weeks later ... all was back to normal.

Both these incidents scared Mom dreadfully.

Oscar was finishing grade 11 when Dad died. The following year he graduated from high school and then was off to university.

The University of Regina Co-op Engineering Program was not a good fit. Training and jobs in carpentry and electronics didn't end up working out for Oscar either. Mom worried about him finding his way in the world. She wanted him to be content and supported him during the many changes he made while searching for the right career path.

Then Oscar enrolled in the journeyman trades certification program at Keyano College in Fort McMurray. He achieved top marks and was hired by the R. Angus Caterpillar company in shipping and receiving. He did an excellent job there and received exceptional performance reviews, earning the respect and friendship of colleagues. He was also active in the employees' union as shop steward—quite remarkable for this soft-spoken, gentle man. He had landed. Mom was so glad for him.

I don't remember why Oscar happened to be visiting me in Saskatoon when I was in university in the fall of 1979. All I *do* remember is that he told me he had been diagnosed with diabetes. He was 29.

When we were growing up, our Grannie Thomas had diabetes. To us kids it really didn't seem like it had much of an impact on her health. We often joked she only seemed to have it when she wanted to; that it was a convenience thing. *If that's what it is like to have diabetes*, I thought, *Oscar will be okay.*

But that's not what it looked like for him. His Type II, adult-onset diabetes was very aggressive. He immediately required insulin injections, and though he worked hard to control his blood sugar through diet, that didn't work. While he wasn't fat, he was broad-shouldered and thickset, and it seemed his body just wouldn't respond properly to treatment.

Mom was extremely worried about Oscar's deteriorating health. Diabetes caused his weight to drop rapidly, his hair to fall out and his vision to diminish. He was so frail. She wished there was something she could do.

On December 6, 1987, Mom and Bordie were in Arizona, as usual, for that time of year. At ten that morning they were heading out with four sets of their friends, all in their respective campers, to drive from Mesa, Arizona to Mexico for a getaway on the Sea of Cortez. When they checked into Organ Pipe Cactus Park near the Mexico border, there was a message for Mom to call her daughter, Karen. It was three-thirty in the afternoon when Karen told Mom, "Oscar is gone."

"What? What happened?" asked Mom.

"He died in his sleep last night."

Mom was in shock. She did not expect this. He was only 37 years old.

When my sister phoned me with the news, at first, I thought she was going to say he had been in a car accident. When she said he had gone to bed, had a heart attack and passed away I couldn't believe it. He was way too young!

On my drive, alone for more than eight hours, from Regina to my brother Ken's in Calgary, I kept hoping I would 'snap out' of a horrible dream. *It can't be true that my brother is gone, just like that,* I thought.

There were moments when I was angry, really angry, at him even though I had never been angry at him even once when he was alive. I yelled out in my car, "Did you know your arteries were clogged? Why didn't you tell us? Maybe the doctors could have done something!"

It was such a shock. We learned heart attacks are a common complication of diabetes. However, Oscar had not informed us that he was at risk. *Maybe he didn't know?* Then again, maybe he did.

My brother Ken met Mom and Bordie at the airport when they arrived in Calgary at five in the morning. Then the four of us drove to Fort McMurray to say our last goodbyes to Oscar and to wind up his estate.

We were surprised to discover that Oscar had already taken care of some of his affairs ... almost as if he was aware of what might happen.

Was it merely a coincidence he'd recently sold his home? Possibly. But how many single, 37-year-olds do you know who take the time to make a will, or who have thought about and expressed their wishes for what they'd like to take place when they die? He had.

It could simply be that, since Dad died when we were young, Oscar realized life could be too short. It could be that because he had diabetes, he guessed that maybe his own life might be cut short. It could also be that he was diagnosed with heart disease and chose not to share it with any of us. Whatever the reason, knowing his wishes certainly helped us, as a family, to deal with planning his service and looking after his estate. The decisions he made in advance gave us guidance and confidence.

Mom mourned the loss of Oscar even more than the loss of Dad. A child dying before a parent is just not right. Mom would have traded places with him if she could. To have a heart attack and die at 67 made more sense than to do so at 37. It was nearly impossible for her to accept his death. The only saving grace was that he was no longer struggling with failing health. She was truly thankful he was saved from suffering.

As Oscar's death was so sudden and there was no opportunity to say final goodbyes, the funeral director encouraged us to write notes to him and put our cards and letters in the casket. It was a simple yet effective way to say goodbye and to tell Oscar all the things we would have liked to say if we'd seen him before he died.

In my note, I wrote how special it was to me that he was at my wedding only four months before, and how I will always smile and feel so fortunate when I remember how he took my husband-to-be aside and told him in no uncertain terms, "You look after my little sister!"

Along with his will, Oscar included a personal letter to Mom, who he appointed his executor. He wrote: 'I want you to gather my friends and relatives for one last get-together to celebrate my passing. There is to be lots of high quality rye, scotch, bourbon, rum, champagne …'

He didn't want us to be sad. He didn't want us to have some sombre event. It helped us to know what he wanted. His invitation to have a celebration and raise a toast to him comforted us in our grief. We were truly touched he had been so caring and thoughtful.

Going through his belongings, we found a small plaque that became a keepsake for Mom. It said, 'When life gives you lemons …. make lemonade.' This saying sums up the approach to life Mom chose, as well as the gift Oscar's careful preparations were for those left behind. Free from making decisions while mourning, we were able to celebrate him.

WHEN LIFE GIVES LEMONS…. MAKE LEMONADE.

For me: I have learned the 'life's too short' lesson many times. In my family, I learned this early, with the passing of my dad and brother. In my husband's family, I learned it yet again.

I had a special relationship with my father-in-law. After he retired, he was talking about writing his autobiography. During one of our conversations, I offered to type up the stories he wanted to share about his experiences serving in the second world war. Unfortunately, before we were able to chronicle his memories, he suffered a stroke and passed away. I regret that I took it for granted he would be with us for years to come. I thought we had lots of time and I am so sorry I was wrong.

When we share our wishes, we make it easier for loved ones should something happen to us. We do not know how much time we have. If we have unfinished business or unsaid thanks to convey, we need to ask, "What are we waiting for?" Getting our affairs in order shows those near and dear to us how much we care.

Your turn to 'take the wheel'

Do you have steps to take, plans to prepare, thanks to express, wishes to **SHARE**? Are there photos, memories, stories or heirlooms you know others would appreciate receiving?

Take a moment to make a list and a plan for what, how and when you will **SHARE**. Then, take the time to do it. You, your family and friends will be genuinely thankful.

. . . .

Three small steps (T.H.X.)
to feel free from regret:

1. **T**ake time to
2. **H**ighlight the positive, and,
3. **X**press gratitude.

WHAT WOULD YOU THINK?

When our health is compromised, choosing to be grateful helps us move forward.

Mom and Bordie were enjoying their nineteenth year as snowbirds. The warm winters and all their activities—swimming, hiking, painting classes, playing cards, eating delicious pot-luck suppers and dancing—kept them feeling young and healthy. It was 1996; Mom was 74 and Bordie was 85.

On Saturday March 9, at the 'Holiday Village Amateur Night', they spent the evening singing along to the music and laughing at the skits. After the show, Mom washed her hair and was putting her curlers in when suddenly she fell to the floor, unconscious. Bordie phoned his brother Vernon and wife Mary, a retired nurse, who lived close by. Mary yelled, "Call 911! We'll be right there!"

The ambulance arrived within minutes and the paramedics took Mom to the Desert Samaritan Hospital a couple of miles away, down South Dobson Road. Mom was admitted to the emergency unit and it was obvious almost immediately that she had suffered a stroke.

The next morning Bordie called to tell me she was in the hospital. Nothing this serious had ever happened to my mom before!

"Is she going to be okay? Should I fly to Phoenix?" I asked anxiously.

"The doctors are doing everything they can," Bordie assured me. "They don't know yet how severely the stroke damaged her brain. They want to stabilize her and then fly her home to Saskatchewan. It's best if you wait."

"Tell her I love her!"

Every day for five days we repeated that conversation. Those were the longest five days of my life. I checked the flight schedules every day. I wanted to be at her side. *She's okay. Bordie and Mary and Vernon and many friends are with her. If I get on a plane, I'll be flying there, and she'll be flying home. Just sit tight.* It was so hard. I felt so helpless.

Finally, on Friday, March 15, Mom's doctor gave the go-ahead for her to fly home. Transportation was arranged by my sister Karen through Mom's insurance company.

Mom and Bordie, with two nurses and two pilots, flew from Mesa to Regina in a private Lear jet. I've never been so happy to see Mom as I was when the door of the plane opened that day. She was lifted onto a gurney and transferred into the ambulance waiting on the tarmac to be taken to the Regina General Hospital.

A day or two later I joked with Mom, "If you wanted to fly in a Lear jet you didn't need to have a stroke!" It took me completely aback when she didn't get the joke. The part of her brain that interprets humour, sarcasm and nuances had been completely scrambled.

Mom was only in the hospital for a few days and then she was moved to the Wascana Rehabilitation Centre for her recovery. There, she went through occupational and physical therapy. When she'd regained her physical strength, she was discharged to live with my husband and me in Regina while she continued speech therapy on an out-patient basis.

At the outset of the speech therapy process, a battery of tests were done to establish a baseline for Mom and then exercises were developed for her based on that. Mom was dedicated and motivated to work hard and slowly her speech improved. When she started to make progress, one of the very first words she was able to say clearly was, "Shit!"

I was so startled, I laughed, but though it struck me as funny, I couldn't help thinking, *what have you done with my mom?* Before her stroke she never swore! However, it was no wonder that word came out. It was so difficult for her to learn to talk again.

Mom was extremely thankful for the competent and caring health professionals in Arizona and Saskatchewan who did everything they could to support her recovery. She was also very grateful her stroke was not worse. She realized she could have died or been confined permanently to a wheelchair, unable to look after herself. Being thankful for these 'saving graces' gave her strength to recover. She never gave up, even when others would have been completely frustrated, embarrassed and just plain mad.

While Mom was with us in Regina, Bordie lived with his daughter in Saskatoon. She recognized her father was developing dementia and would need more care than my mom, post-stroke, would be able to handle.

His daughter arranged for supports to be put in place before Mom and Bordie returned to Tisdale. When Bordie's condition worsened, arrangements were made for him to be cared for in a facility in Saskatoon, where he passed away in October 1998 at the age of 87. Until their health challenges, Mom and Bordie shared a wonderful second marriage.

Mom lived with a speech impairment for the rest of her life, but with a grateful mindset, and determination not to give up, she continued to make progress, relearning one word at a time as her brain kept healing and creating new pathways.

It took a long time for Mom to get my joke about her having a stroke so she could fly in a Lear jet. When she did, we both had a good laugh. I was thankful to have my mom back.

For me: When I was 46, I required major surgery. I was thankful for the skilled and caring team of professionals at Calgary's Women's Health Centre, grateful my biopsy results showed my tumour was benign and relieved my recovery was speedy.

While my surgery immediately plunged me into menopause, I soon realized that there was an upside to the hot flashes that followed. To this day, if I feel one coming on, I stop and take stock of what I'm doing as my 'personal heat waves' are a sure signal that I'm feeling stress. Being aware when stress is triggered has allowed me to consciously identify what's going on and take action to deal with it. That's an unexpected bonus I've come to appreciate.

When our health is compromised, choosing to be grateful helps us move forward. Things we take for granted can change suddenly and dramatically. What we do after that determines what we're made of. Finding ways to say 'thanks' eases our long road to recovery.

Your turn to 'take the wheel'

Appreciation is conveyed when you simply **SAY** thanks. Thanks can be expressed personally to one individual, by raising a toast to many, or in the form of offering grace or 'gratitudes' before a meal.

One of my personal favourite toasts is in Gaelic. It's 'slàinte mhath' (pronounced 'slancha-va'), which means 'good health' and it is offered as thanks to the host of an event and other guests.

Think about, and note below, who—individuals, groups or a higher power—you will **SAY** 'thanks' to or list the kinds of occasions when you will give thanks.

Three small steps (T.H.X.)
to feel free from regret:

1. Take time to
2. Highlight the positive, and.
3. Xpress gratitude.

WHAT WOULD YOU NEED?

When we choose a place to live that meets our needs, we feel younger, happier, better.

Deciding if, or when, it's time to move out of their own home is one of the most difficult decisions many people have to make as they age. Many are reluctant, or even down-right against, considering options. To some, moving out of their home feels like giving up, of no longer being in control and of being old and frail. But as we get older, many of us need a little help to take care of ourselves or matters around the house.

Thankfully, my mom didn't worry about this at all! Mom was 81 when she called and left me a message. I can still hear her voice, "It's Mom. I'm coming to Calgary forever and ever." Maybe the changes she experienced throughout her life helped her realize there was no harm in trying something new. Maybe her innate sense of adventure allowed her to believe she would have a richer life if she was living with others her age. Maybe her willingness to be open to possibilities let her feel confident she would still be in the driver's seat if she made this choice for herself. Whatever it was, she moved to Calgary in 2003, where she was not only closer to me but also to my oldest brother Ken and his family.

Mom always loved Calgary. In 1968, my parents took Oscar and me on a terrific trip to visit Ken, who was studying aviation at the Southern Alberta Institute of Technology. A cherished memory I have of that trip was when Ken took us to the top of the Husky Tower (now Calgary Tower) for breakfast. As we were getting ready to leave the restaurant, Dad noticed his hat was missing. Those were the days when a man wasn't dressed unless he wore a hat. Luckily, since the top of the tower was a revolving restaurant, it wasn't long until his hat came back. Every time after that whenever Mom saw the Calgary Tower, she thought fondly of Dad.

It was up to Mom and me to find a place for her to live. To help us determine which of the various seniors' homes would be the best for her, we made a list of amenities important to Mom. Then we took tours, asked lots of questions and eventually fell in love with the Fountains of Mission Retirement Residence.

Mom moved in on the day it opened. We called her new home the 'five-star model' of retirement residences. With lovely surroundings, gourmet meals, delightful staff and friendly residents, all of Mom's needs were met. And the promise of additional care (medication assistance, tray service when ill and more) whenever she might require it made the Fountains an especially attractive choice for her and our family.

Contrary to misconceptions some people have about retirement home living, when Mom decided to move into a retirement residence, it *increased* her independence. All her day-to-day essentials were looked after, which not only took the pressure of caregiving off family members but allowed Mom to save her energy for 'the good stuff'!

Since Mom volunteered to deliver the Fountains' weekly calendar of events to residents, she knew what day trips and activities were scheduled. That way she was always the first one signed up for everything she wanted to do.

Inspired by the movie, *Calendar Girls*, the Fountains decided to create its own calendar and raise money for charity, as well as promote itself as a retirement residence. Mom immediately volunteered to be part of this campaign, which turned out to be very successful. It attracted lots of press, with headlines reading, 'Seniors take it off for charity' and the like. For Mom, it was such fun—not to mention it was for a good cause, which she valued.

Seniors take it off for charity

ALEX FRAZER-HARRISON
FOR NEIGHBOURS

For Calgary's own Calendar Girls (and guys), doffing their duds for a series of photos was all in good fun — and all for the sake of raising money for charity.

For the last several years, the Fountains of Mission Retirement Residence on 25th Avenue S.W. has spotlighted some of its residents in their own calendar, beautifully photographed and sold to raise money for local charities.

The idea was inspired by the popular film, Calendar Girls, in which a group of older women decides to pose nude for a calendar to raise money for a hospital.

Mom was 82 when she posed in a top hat, tails and fishnet stockings. 'Yes, those legs *are* insured by Lloyd's of London!' said the caption below the photo of her looking spectacular. It was obvious from the way she was beaming that she felt alive and just a touch sassy!

Photo Credit, Susan Warner
Photography, Calgary

The following year she dressed as a go-go dancer, but though most 83-year-old women would be thrilled to look as good as she did, she didn't really care for her costume.

At the age of 85, she decided not to be in the calendar again … until the theme was announced: 'The Classics—Cars, Gals & Guys'. My husband's 1964 Galaxy convertible was selected to appear in the 2008 calendar, and after that, wild horses could not have kept Mom from being the one in the driver's seat. That's her on the cover of this book!

For Mom, choosing a retirement residence was the way to go. It kept her healthy, active and full of life. She also made some fine friends: Mary and Dick, who moved in on the first day like she did; Reva, formerly from Saskatoon; Nancy, who shared Mom's love of knitting; almost 100-year-old Margie; and, retired nun, Thérèse, to name a few. Retirement home living not only freed Mom from chores such as grocery shopping and cooking, but she never had to eat her meals alone.

I vividly remember the time we returned to her suite after being away on one of our trips and Mom remarked, "It's nice to be home." I knew then Mom had made the right choice to move into the Fountains of Mission.

For me: When Mom was living with us in Regina after her stroke, one fall day I went home from work just after noon expecting to have lunch with her. When I arrived to find an empty house, I couldn't believe it! *What happened to her?!*

The first thing I did was reach for the phone to call for help, and I saw the light blinking on our answering machine. After listening to the Safeway store manager's message about his staff coming to Mom's aid and calling the ambulance, I cried tears of joy and relief!

Afterwards, it was my pleasure to spread the word of this story with such a happy ending by writing to our local daily newspaper, the Regina LeaderPost.

Ida-Jean McIntyre has some very kind words for the staff at the Safeway store at Albert Street and 25th Avenue.

Her mother was shopping there on Sept. 6 when she felt faint and asked for help.

Responding immediately were cashier **Shelley Leader** and courtesy clerk **Dan Johnson**, who, she adds, wants to become an emergency medical technician.

An ambulance was called and a heart pacemaker was implanted within days. Ida-Jean reports her mother is doing fine.

The staff's good work didn't stop there.

Right after the incident, Ida-Jean writes, store manager Ed Farias "called and left a phone message for me that was very sensitive and calm, which prevented a sense of panic in me."

And Shelley called that evening to check on how her mom was doing.

This kindness is why Ida-Jean wrote a letter of thanks to the staff involved and to Canada Safeway's head office in Calgary.

"I was just incredibly impressed by the service and the care they provided," she says.

"It made a tough situation just a little bit better."

When we choose a place to live that meets our needs, we feel younger, happier, better. We can influence others, too, by telling good news stories of delightful experiences and encounters.

Your turn to 'Take the wheel'

Are there people in your community who have assisted you who you wish to acknowledge? Consider thanking them by writing a letter to a newspaper or posting a note on social media.

When you **TELL** the world about your gratitude, the enlightening energy you generate will spread. Begin with expressing your thanks publicly for one person or experience and see for yourself how good it feels to you and others.

· ·

Three small steps (T.H.X.)
to feel free from regret:

1. Take time to
2. Highlight the positive, and,
3. Xpress gratitude.

How will you feel?

When it's our final farewell,
if we have lived gratefully, we will
feel free from regret.

Late in August 2010, I arrived at Mom's place and found her right hand, lower legs and ankles visibly swollen. She was also congested, had a sore throat and a dry cough. I called her doctor, but the first available appointment was not until the end of the week.

Dr. Wheeler had been Mom's doctor since she moved to Calgary seven years before. She insisted she didn't want to see anyone but her own doctor. She trusted him and so did I. He was an excellent doctor; he even made house calls to visit his patients.

Her insistence on seeing Dr. Wheeler was a dilemma for me. I didn't know what I should do. *Does she need to see a doctor right away, or can it wait? Should I take her to emergency?*

We debated this for a while and finally agreed to go see Dr. Wheeler on Friday. Until then, we asked the Fountains of Mission nurses to check in on her.

The next day, Mom was supposed to see a play, but it was cancelled so she spent the day in bed. In the afternoon, I called the nurses at the Fountains and arranged for them to take Mom soup and tea for supper, as well as to check in on her. One of her very favourite nurses, Venice, was on shift that evening. Just before midnight my home phone rang. It was Venice. She was very concerned about Mom and thought I should come over right away.

I drove to the Fountains and let myself in to Mom's suite. When I went into her bedroom, she asked, "Why are you here?"

I told her Venice had called me and I added, "I heard there's a pajama party." Then I curled up on her couch and told her, "I'm here if you need me."

Mom had a very restless sleep. Her breathing was laboured, and she was obviously uncomfortable. At six-thirty in the morning, she woke up in distress, clutching her chest, "It hurts! It hurts!" she wailed.

I was sure she was having a heart attack! I pressed the alarm for the nurse. Venice came right away and called the ambulance. The emergency medical technicians transported Mom to Foothills Hospital where they diagnosed pneumonia. The fluid on her lungs had caused the swelling and severe pain. It also started a roller coaster of failing health.

At first, Mom's pneumonia started to clear up. Then she suffered a significant setback and we thought we were going to lose her—she had contracted thrush. As her body weakened, the doctors did what they could to treat her, but ultimately the medical staff said it was up to Mom to decide whether she was going to get better or not. I was extremely worried. She wasn't eating, and she looked so frail.

Then, one morning she pointed at the boiled egg on her breakfast tray and said, "I'm going to eat that. I've had enough. I'm going to get better."

By the end of September, she was well enough to return home to the Fountains and it seemed like she was going to be okay.

However, in November, when Dr. Wheeler made a house call to check on Mom, within minutes of walking into her suite he ordered an ambulance. Back to Foothills Hospital she went, for a week this time. Congestive heart failure was confirmed, medication was prescribed, and she returned home to the Fountains—back to normal once again.

The following March, I went to visit Mom on my birthday and found her so ill I called the ambulance. This time, she was rushed to the Rockyview Hospital for a blood transfusion. She was admitted for an overnight stay, and all day between tests and treatment, we reminisced about being in the hospital as we had been 51 years before, when she gave birth to me.

At the end of April, Mom started experiencing sharp, shooting pain in her legs. Ultrasound confirmed it was not a blood clot. Her muscles would simply run out of oxygen sometimes, even when she was sitting. She couldn't bear it—it hurt so much whenever it happened. We learned it was called 'rest pain'.

In May, she developed an arterial wound that would not heal due to her poor circulation and so we made several trips to Calgary's Sheldon M. Chumir Wound Clinic and to Rockyview Hospital for bone and blood scans. Nothing helped.

But more than the escalating number and frequency of medical problems, the clearest indication of Mom's state of health was when I invited her to come with me on a business trip to Ottawa and she replied, "Oh, I've done that." Until that point in time, nothing could have stopped her from travelling wherever, whenever she was given the opportunity.

On Sunday, June 5, I flew to Ottawa. That night, the Fountains of Mission nurses called my brother Ken to tell him that Mom was experiencing excruciating pain. She was taken by ambulance to the Rockyview Hospital.

Upon my return that Wednesday, I went straight to the hospital and walked into her room. I leaned down close to her. She opened her eyes, looked at me, and said, "Oh, it's you."

Those would be the last words she spoke. In three days, she was gone. At last, Mom was free of pain and at peace.

For me: I did not know until Mom passed away what I would feel. Even though I was as prepared and ready as possible, her absence left a huge hole in my heart. For a very long time after, when I'd return home from a business trip, I would automatically pick up the phone to call her before catching myself and remembering, *she's not there.*

I still miss her dearly.

While I am profoundly thankful to have had such an admirable role model of a mom, and I firmly believe gratitude is an essential element of being healthy and happy, the power of gratitude does not guarantee a completely regret-free life.

One of my regrets is that I did not know I would write this book before Mom passed away, so I never had a chance to let her know. However, I find comfort in imagining how she would have reacted if she did know. I can see and hear and feel her tremendous delight; and that allows me to feel free from that regret.

When it's our final farewell, if we have lived gratefully, we will feel free from regret. That was the way it was for Mom. I believe it will be that way for me and it can be for you, too.

Final Thoughts

Even though Mom lost her two husbands, her son, her farmhouse to a fire, her speech to a stroke and the quality of her health for the last ten months of her life, she lived with a remarkably optimistic outlook. While Mom couldn't change the less than perfect parts of her life, she *did* change the way she felt about them. She was always able to find something to be grateful for, albeit not always right in the middle of the worst of times. Sometimes it took hindsight.

Her 89 years were also full of marvelous moments and memories. She loved her 'two men' (that's what she called her husbands after her stroke left her with a speech impairment), her winters in Arizona, the joy of painting, her active eighties in a retirement residence, the warmth of her friendships and, above all, her family.

For me, I have learned that at each fork in my road, it is up to me to choose the way to go. I have found the best road to feeling less regret is the one paved with gratitude.

What are the forks in the road of your life? What's holding you back? What are you waiting for? May living gratefully be the way you 'take the wheel' on your life's journey towards feeling fortunate and free from regret.

Science Says

I'm not suggesting we must be grateful for everything in our lives. In fact, that may be practically impossible. And, there's no need to feel guilty if we are not thankful. However, two decades of research suggest that the more we choose to be grateful, the better the benefits are for us.

Below are some of the best research examples I have discovered to date.

The Greater Good Science Center at UC Berkeley issued a white paper, *The Science of Gratitude*, in May 2018. I found it to be an excellent, comprehensive overview of the benefits of gratitude. If you're interested, you will find a link to it on my website: www.thegratefulway.ca

Three separate studies have demonstrated that counting blessings instead of burdens is an effective way to enhance quality of life (Emmons and McCullough 2003).

Considerable evidence shows that gratitude builds social resources by strengthening relationships and promoting prosocial actions. (Emmons & Mishra 2011).

Science has demonstrated that gratitude enhances peace of mind, reduces rumination and alleviates depressive symptoms (Liang, Chen, Li, Wu, Wang, Zheng, & Zeng, 2018).

Expressing gratitude strengthens our resilience and promotes health and well-being (Sirois 2019; Lyubomirsky, S., & Della Porta, M. D. 2010).

Research reveals gratitude increases our self-control, which helps us stick to the 'better choice' for our long-term health, financial future, and well-being (DeSteno et al., 2014).

Being grateful improves self-esteem. When we feel grateful, we often view ourselves as benefiting from another person's generosity, leading us to feel valued (Lin, 2015).

Gratitude has been linked to psychological, or 'eudaimonic' wellbeing, which is a sense that one's life has meaning and that a person is living their life to the fullest (Wood et al., 2010).

Expressing gratitude increases our empathy and can decrease our self-centeredness, making us more likely to share with others (DeSteno, Bartlett, Baumann, Williams, & Dickens, 2010).

A Harvard Medical School and Massachusetts General Hospital study found acute coronary syndrome patients experienced greater improvements in health-related quality of life when they approached recovery with gratitude and optimism (Millstein, Celano, Beale, Beach, Suarez, Belcher, ... & Huffman, 2016).

And, while daily expressions of gratitude are often recommended, at least one study has found that heartfelt, intermittent, intentional practice is better than constant passive, automated expressions of thankfulness (Lyubomirsky, Sheldon, & Schkade, 2005).

For links to the above studies and the latest research, please see: www.thegratefulway.ca

Ten Ways to Express Gratitude

COUNT	CALL
SHOW	VISIT
SEND	GIVE
WRITE	SHARE
SAY	TELL

Three small steps (T.H.X.)
to feel free from regret:

1. Take time to
2. Highlight the positive, and,
3. Xpress gratitude.

Book Club Conversation Starters

1. Do you see yourself (or someone you know) in one or more of the chapters? If so, which one(s) and why?

2. What does gratitude mean to you? Has reading this book changed the way you think about gratitude in any way? If so, how?

3. Do you have regrets? Do you agree that living gratefully can help you feel free from regret? Why or why not?

4. Do you already actively practice gratitude? Has reading this book inspired or motivated you to take action to express gratitude? If so, specifically, what will you do as a result of reading this book?

5. Are any of the 'Ten Ways to Express Gratitude' suggested at the end of the chapters 'new to you' ideas that you might try? Are there any other ways to express gratitude that you would add?

6. Will you take the three small steps of T.H.X.? Do you think they are small? Simple? Easy? Difficult?

    IJ would love to hear your stories. If you are willing to share, please don't hesitate to connect with IJ. You'll find several ways to contact her on her website: www.thegratefulway.ca

    Thank you!

For more inspiration view IJ.'s Talk:
Feel Regret-free with Gratitude
on TEDx.com

About the Author

Like you, gratitude aficionado, speaker and writer IJ (Ida-Jean) McIntyre has experienced personal triumphs, struggles and regrets. Intrigued by her mom's ability to address adversity as well as embrace opportunity, IJ wondered, *how was Mom so positive and optimistic? Was she born that way, or was she one-of-a-kind? What can be learned from the way she lived her life?*

Writing this book, IJ discovered we can *choose* to have a thankful mindset, we can learn to express appreciation, and that living gratefully can free us from feelings of regret.

A member of the Canadian Association of Professional Speakers, IJ talks with women, especially those on the upside of 55, wherever they gather to share the simple yet powerful 'whys and ways' of living gratefully. Her thought-provoking, upbeat and often amusing presentations are a unique blend of heart-spun wisdom and real-life research that encourage women to live more thankfully using her inspiring philosophy of the three small steps of T.H.X.!

A small-town Saskatchewan upbringing, two university degrees, fifteen years of public service, five years of corporate human resource experience and fifteen years of facilitating retirement life planning workshops have given IJ the insight to help people explore their lives, make plans and take positive actions that are right for them.

IJ is certified in two personality temperament tools, holds two retirement life planning designations, has served on two national boards of directors and has had articles featured in the National Post, Vancouver Sun, Calgary Herald and Toronto Star.

Described by some as 'relentlessly positive', IJ loves road trips, roller coasters, and reading mystery thrillers.

IJ invites you to nurture your own grateful attitude by going to her website, www.thegratefulway.ca, where you can:

- Print your own copy of the 'Ten Ways to Express Gratitude' mini-poster on page 70.

- Print one or more of the 'Your turn to take the wheel' contemplation and commitment Sheets at the end of each of the chapters.

- Contact IJ or connect with her through social media.

- Subscribe to receive IJ's inspirational blog posts.

- Share the ways that you express gratitude and your stories of how you've experienced the power of gratitude.

- Share your Book Club Conversations.

- Find links to the latest gratitude research study results.

- Check out exclusive discounts for bulk orders of this book.

- Learn more about IJ's speaking schedule and arrange to have her speak to your group.

- Join IJ in living 'the grateful way'!